The Thinking Girl's Treasury of Real Princesses

Hatshepsut of Egypt

© **2010 Goosebottom Books LLC**

All rights reserved

Series editor **Shirin Yim Bridges**
Consulting editor **Amy Novesky**
Copy editor **Jennifer Fry**
Book design **Jay Mladjenovic**

Typeset mainly in Papyrus and Volkswagen TS
Illustrations rendered in pen and watercolor

Some photographs used under Creative Commons Attribution/Share Alike license
http://creativecommons.org/licenses/by-sa/3.0/

Manufactured in Singapore

Library of Congress PCN 2010903613

First Edition   10 9 8 7 6 5 4 3 2 1

Goosebottom Books LLC
710 Portofino Lane, Foster City CA 94404

www.goosebottombooks.com

For Tiegan and Alena, the original Thinking Girl
and the real Fairy-Monkey Princess.

~ Shirin Yim Bridges ~

For my family and friends.

~ Albert Nguyen ~

The Thinking Girl's Treasury of Real Princesses

Hatshepsut of Egypt

Artemisia of Caria

Sorghaghtani of Mongolia

Qutlugh Terkan Khatun of Kirman

Isabella of Castile

Nur Jahan of India

Hatshepsut of Egypt

By Shirin Yim Bridges | Illustrated by Albert Nguyen

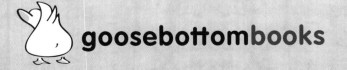
goosebottombooks

She was called what?!

The names in this book can be hard to pronounce, and dictionaries often don't help — trying to work out dictionary pronunciation symbols can be like trying to read hieroglyphics!

Here are most of the unusual names encountered in this book, with a rough-and-easy guide to pronunciation. You can also hear many of these names pronounced on the website www.howjsay.com.

(Try it, it's neat.)

Hatshepsut	hat•shep•soot
Tutankhamun	toot•an•cah•mun
Djeser-Djeseru	je•zer•je•zer•roo
Pharaoh	fair•oh
Thutmose	tut•mose
Artemisia	ah•tim•mis•sia
Byblos	bib•bloss
Kalasiris	kal•ah•se•ris
Usekh	you•sec
Uraeus	you•ray•es
Nemes	nem•mees
Shendyt	shen•dit
Hieroglyphs	high•ro•gliffs

Hatshepsut of Egypt

When explorers first chipped a hole through the wall and shined a light into Tutankhamun's tomb, breaking the darkness after thousands of years, everything it touched glinted with gold and gleamed with silver. Wherever the torchlight fell, it set fire to gems and lit the sparkle of precious stones. Never before had the world seen such treasure. The boy-king who was found buried amidst these luxuries would become one of the most famous names in history.

But a less-famous princess had accumulated a lot of the wealth found in that tomb. This princess built one of Egypt's most magnificent temples, the *Djeser-Djeseru*, in the Valley of the Kings, not far from where she built her tomb.

The Valley of the Kings. But wasn't she a girl? Shouldn't she have been buried in the Valley of the Queens? Well, no. Because the princess we're talking about was Hatshepsut, Egypt's first female *king* or pharaoh.

Sadly, nothing remains of Hatshepsut's palaces. But marked on this map are some monuments erected by Hatshepsut, which you can still visit, around the city of Luxor.

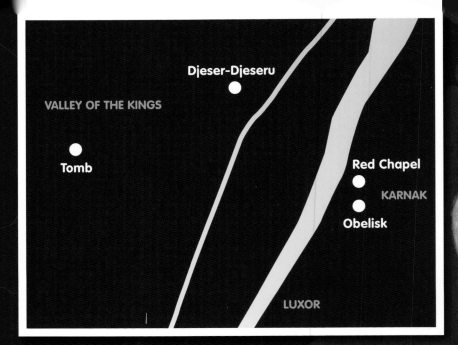

When she lived

This timeline shows when the other princesses in The Thinking Girl's Treasury of Real Princesses once lived.

1500BC	500BC	1200AD	1300AD	1400AD	1600AD
Hatshepsut of Egypt	Artemisia of Caria	Sorghaghtani of Mongolia	Qutlugh Terkan Khatun	Isabella of Castile	Nur Jahan of India

Her story

Hatshepsut was born around 1500 BC. That's almost three and a half thousand years ago — 350 times longer than you've been alive, if you're ten years old. The daughter of Thutmose I, a great pharaoh of Egypt (the "I" means "The First"; as you'll see, there were many Thutmoses after him), Hatshepsut was her father's favorite, and he often kept her by his side while he went about the complicated business of government. He liked the way Hatshepsut paid close attention to what he said, and how she learned quickly, and over the years he taught Hatshepsut many things about running a large country like Egypt.

Loved by her father, growing up in a beautiful palace in a sun-soaked land, life should have been good for this princess. But Hatshepsut was saddened by death. First her sister and then her two brothers died, one after the other, from unknown causes. The palace, whose stately columns and painted walls once echoed with the footsteps and laughter of royal children, fell mournfully silent.

As a father, Thutmose I was heartbroken, but as Pharaoh, he also had a problem on his hands. In Ancient Egypt, women rarely inherited the throne. Like most of the world at that time, the Egyptians thought that men made better rulers. (The Ancient Greeks were even worse. They didn't think women should even be allowed to own their homes! But more on that in the book about Artemisia of Caria.) So, who would inherit the country now that the royal princes were dead?

▶ The Ancient Egyptians preserved the lungs, liver, intestines, and stomach separately in four canopic jars like this one.

▲ Royal mummies were placed in coffins elaborately carved and painted to look like the person.

In the Egyptian Museum in Cairo, you can still see Tutankhamun's golden throne, carved with portraits of him and Smenkhkare.

The Pharaoh's solution was to marry Hatshepsut to her half-brother, one of his sons from a non-royal wife. This half-royal son could then inherit the throne, married to the fully royal princess. It sounds awful to us now, but it was quite common in Ancient Egypt to marry your sister or brother. So the marriage went ahead, and when Thutmose I died a few years later, Hatshepsut's brother/husband inherited the throne as Pharaoh Thutmose II.

It seems that Thutmose II was a sickly man. Hatshepsut, who was healthy, bright, and knew about government from her father, began to play an unusually large part in ruling the country. When Thutmose II died shortly afterwards, leaving only a very young son by another wife to inherit the throne, it came as no surprise to anyone that the court recognized Hatshepsut as Regent (the real ruler behind the throne).

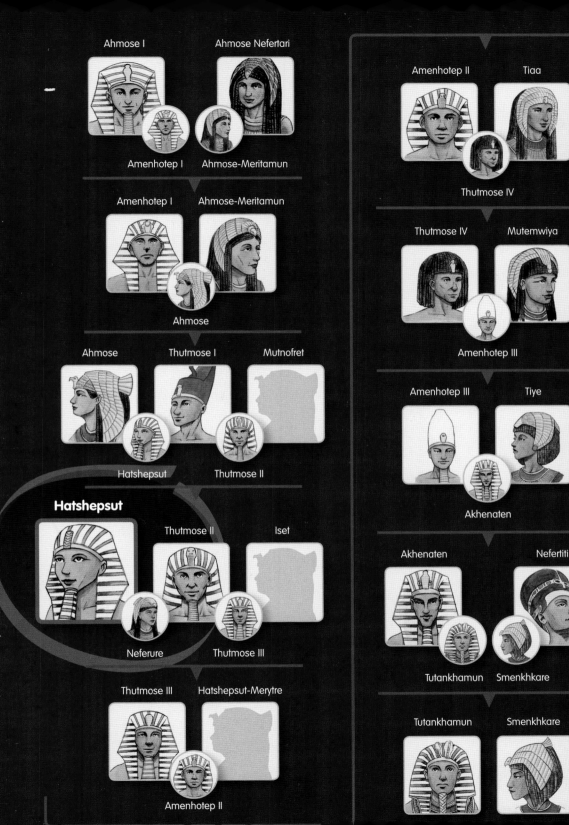

Ahmose I — Ahmose Nefertari
Amenhotep I — Ahmose-Meritamun

Amenhotep I — Ahmose-Meritamun
Ahmose

Ahmose — Thutmose I — Mutnofret
Hatshepsut — Thutmose II

Hatshepsut

Hatshepsut — Thutmose II — Iset
Neferure — Thutmose III

Thutmose III — Hatshepsut-Merytre
Amenhotep II

Amenhotep II — Tiaa
Thutmose IV

Thutmose IV — Mutemwiya
Amenhotep III

Amenhotep III — Tiye
Akhenaten

Akhenaten — Nefertiti
Tutankhamun — Smenkhkare

Tutankhamun — Smenkhkare

The fabulous 18th Dynasty

Egypt's 18th Dynasty was its most glamorous. Take a look! You'll find most of the famous pharaohs and queens here. And all of them were related in some way to Hatshepsut.

As you can see, marrying your brother or sister was quite common!

Note: There is still disagreement among historians about some connections.

What she wore

Hatshepsut probably spent most of her time dressed like any other Egyptian queen or princess. Historians think that she only donned her pharaoh's garb for official occasions. (Some think that she never donned it at all, but was only depicted that way in paintings and wall carvings.) It would have taken guts for a woman to face a crowd dressed as a pharaoh. But guts is one thing Hatshepsut had.

Vulture cap Symbol of the goddess Nekhbet, this was the most common headdress of queens

Usekh Jeweled collar worn over the shoulders, made of precious stones set in gold

Kalasiris Long, close-fitting linen robe, usually white; its fineness and transparency were a sign of wealth, with queens wearing some of the most see-through robes of all!

Uraeus Royal crown in the form of an upright spitting cobra, symbol of the goddess Wadjet, protector of the Pharaoh and Egypt

Nemes Royal striped head cloth

False metal beard Sign of sovereignty

Shendyt Egyptian kilt

What *did* surprise everyone was what happened only two years later: to the blast of trumpets, and before the bowed heads of Egypt's highest priests and officials, Hatshepsut was declared Pharaoh, King of Egypt! This had never happened before. Although women had sometimes ruled Egypt as queens and regents, no woman had ever been declared Pharaoh.

To make it very clear that she was now Pharaoh and no longer just Queen, Hatshepsut began dressing as a pharaoh on official occasions — in the men's clothes that were the symbols of supreme power in Egypt. Imagine the reaction when Hatshepsut first stood before her people in a pharaoh's blue and white striped head cloth, wearing a man's short kilt instead of a woman's long robes, her breasts bare underneath her heavy gold collar, a false beard strapped to her chin! The Egyptians were a very conservative people, and they must have wondered what on earth their lovely princess was doing. (Luckily, they would have another 22 years to get used to this.)

As Pharaoh of Egypt, Hatshepsut could have taken the attitude that Egypt, with its temples and palaces, great cities, industrious villages and fertile farmlands, had everything it needed. Or she could have followed in the footsteps of her father and waged war to add spoils and booty to Egypt's riches. Instead, Hatshepsut concentrated on establishing trading relationships with many countries, both near and far. And this trade would make Egypt richer and more powerful than it had ever been.

From Byblos, the country we now call Lebanon, new trade brought Egypt great stores of timber. Timber was very valuable because Egypt, although fertile, was a land of few trees. From Sinai, the area now home to Israelis and Palestinians, trade brought horses — a relatively new animal for the Egyptians, and one that would prove useful in war. (The armies of Egypt would one day be famous for their horse-drawn chariots.)

What she ate

Egypt's source of wealth was the Nile. The land that spread out on both sides of the river was kept fertile by floods that left behind new layers of mud and silt every year. Wheat, barley, fruits, and vegetables grew in this rich soil; there was plenty of fodder for cows and goats; and the river provided fish, turtles, frogs, ducks, and geese for the royal table. (Although you probably don't eat turtles or frogs, in many parts of the world people find them quite delicious.) Egypt grew rich because it was the bread-basket of the ancient world — Hatshepsut had valuable grain to trade on her expeditions. But, life for the average Egyptian was not luxurious. Their daily diet was coarse bread (sometimes so full of desert sand that it ground down their teeth!) and beer, and in bad years when the Nile did not flood, Egypt was plagued by famine.

▲ Egyptian boats like this were built to travel and trade on the Nile, not on the ocean.

But Hatshepsut's most famous trading expedition was the journey to the mysterious land of Punt (we are not sure exactly where it was, but it might have been on the Horn of Africa or somewhere in Arabia). The Egyptians were not ocean sailors, so for them this was like going to the moon. Hatshepsut must have shivered with excitement under her pharaoh's headdress as she stood on the dock watching her five ships, each laden with gold and manned by 30 rowers, setting sail for seas where few Egyptians had ventured before.

The booty that was eventually brought home in exchange for this gold was carefully recorded on the walls of Hatshepsut's temple, Djeser-Djeseru. In intricate detail you can still see pictures of apes and greyhounds, leopard skins and jewels, ebony and ivory, being unloaded from the ships.

On Hatshepsut's personal shopping list were 31 potted myrrh trees. Myrrh was extremely rare and valuable. She had the trees planted on a terrace at Djeser-Djeseru, and dedicated them to her father. Proudly and lovingly she wrote: "I have made him a Punt in his garden, as he commanded me... It is big enough for him to walk abroad in."

▶ Pictures of Hatshepsut's expedition to Punt can still be seen on the walls of Djeser-Djeseru.

You can still visit Hatshepsut's magnificent temple, Djeser-Djeseru, near the Valley of the Kings in Egypt.

What's interesting is that everything brought back from Punt was a luxury. Unlike most trading expeditions, Hatshepsut's great venture did not bring back grain, or oil, or cloth, or food or necessities of any kind. The Egyptians must have had no need.

During Hatshepsut's long reign of 22 years, Egypt enjoyed relative peace, stored and sold surplus grain, and grew wealthy. Egypt's cities and temples flourished. Egyptian architecture achieved dazzling heights. And treasures piled up — a tiny fraction of which, finding its way into Tutankhamun's tomb, would one day amaze the world. For all this, Egypt had to thank the king who was born a princess.

A lingering mystery

Now, you may be asking yourself, "If Hatshepsut was such a great ruler, why haven't I heard more about her? Why isn't she as famous as Tutankhamun?" Part of the reason is that someone tried to wipe Hatshepsut out of history. After her death, many of her statues were destroyed and many hieroglyphs about her deeds were chiseled off the walls.

For a long time, the theory was that Hatshepsut had been a wicked stepmother who'd stolen the throne from her stepson. When Hatshepsut died and Thutmose III became Pharaoh on his own (he had never actually been kicked off the throne, they had been joint pharaohs all along), he took his revenge and had many records of Hatshepsut wiped out.

What makes this unlikely is that Thutmose III was already powerful when Hatshepsut was still alive. While Hatshepsut devoted herself to her trade and building projects, Thutmose III commanded Egypt's vast armies. He went on to become one of the fiercest

© Walwyn/Creative Commons

▶ Some defaced monuments to Hatshepsut. If you look closely, you can see her outline in the lighter chiselled-off area in the photo of the wall.

© Keith Schengili-Roberts/Creative Commons

© Tom Chandler/Creative Commons

and most warlike pharaohs in Egyptian history. Would a great military leader with the might of the armies behind him have simmered for years in silence?

Another theory was that Hatshepsut had fooled the Egyptians into thinking she was a man. When they found out, they were so angry at having been duped that they tried to wipe her out of history.

This is also unlikely since Hatshepsut — as princess, queen, and regent — had a very public life. (There's also the fact that a pharaoh's costume exposes the breasts. Surely Hatshepsut's would have raised a few questions?)

Historians really don't have any firm answers. The general thinking now is that at some later date, the conservative Egyptians thought it would be better not to admit to having had a female king — even if it was one who'd made them fabulously rich. So, most of Hatshepsut's records were destroyed.

Pharaoh Hatshepsut died on January 16, 1458 BC, probably from a blood infection. She was around 42 years old. She was buried with the full rites of a pharaoh in the Valley of the Kings, next to her father, Thutmose I.